SHIRTLESS STEPHEN
and the Children's Crusade
version for voices, piano and percussion

Poems by Peter Porter

Geoffrey Burgon (2002)

dip our horns, they'll take the toss, From Shirt-less Ste-phen of the Cross.

Great

bish-ops here in fer-tile France Will bless each pace of our ad-vance; The man who'll lead the bold at-tack, He

The man who'll lead the bold at-tack, He

4

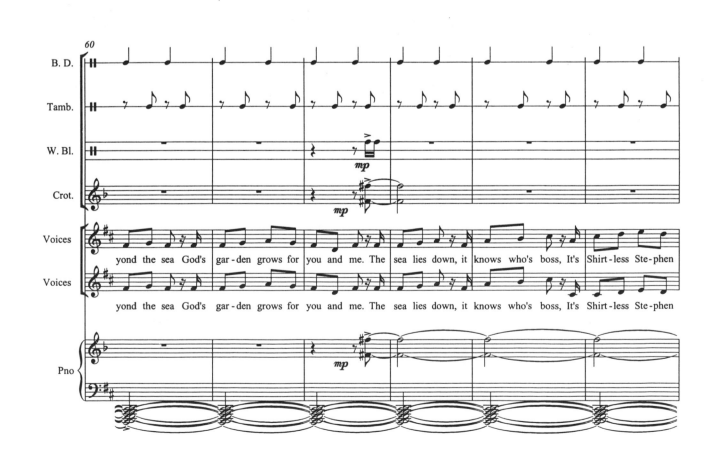

Voices: light, And like the wil-low in its sleep A mo-ther hangs her head to weep.

Voices: The ta-ma-rind shakes out its leaves, And hides the breeze in-side its sleeves. There

Voices: Sha-ron's pool is glassed with dust and Tan-cred's sword drops flakes of rust. Come

Voices: back, you days of God-frey bold, Re-store the gra-cious Age of Gold, And Ac-re, Ga-za, An-ti-

Voices: och, Re-joice a-gain by Zi-on's Rock.

3

Now Stephen puts his shirt back on

Now Ste - phen puts his shirt back on And teach - es you a - no - ther song. The

e - ne - mies of God must fall When chil - dren march a - gainst their wall. From An - ti - christ comes

har‑vest, bones; The chil‑dren cry a‑cross the sea What was, what is, what still must be.

har‑vest, bones; The chil‑dren cry a‑cross the sea What was, what is, what still must be.

Stephen's letter from The Virgin Mary

To my be-lo-ved ser-vant, Ste-phen of the sweet skin: Love your

mo-ther who blea-ches wash-ing on the stones of St. Cloud:___ you must wear___ your wool-ly vest___

when the wind is high, but when God's sun shines, show your cut-tle bo-dy to the world.

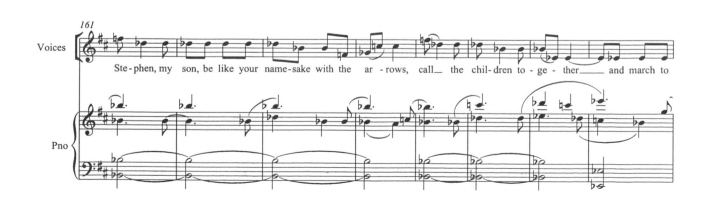

Ste-phen, my son, be like your name-sake with the ar-rows, call___ the chil-dren to-ge-ther___ and march to

5
Stephen's Final Resolve

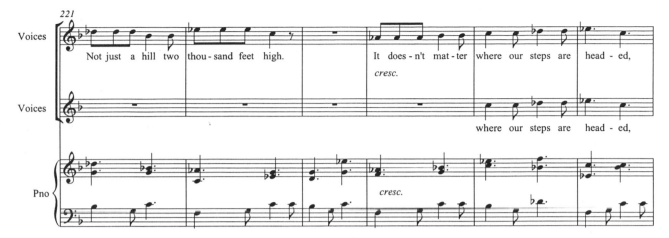

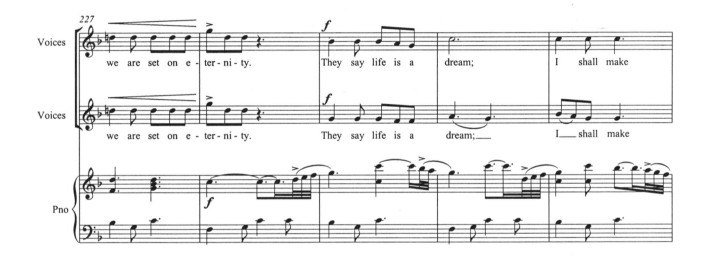

Lypiatt 25 5 02

Crusaders' March

In Outremer beyond the sea
God's garden grows for you and me.
The sea lies down, it knows who's boss,
It's Shirtless Stephen of the Cross.

From harboured Tyre to Galilee,
From storming peaks to silver sea,
We'll dip our horns, they'll take the toss,
From Shirtless Stephen of the Cross.

Great Bishops here in fertile France
Will bless each pace of our advance;
The man who'll lead the bold attack,
He wears no shirt upon his back.

And you will follow him to Hell,
The Saracens shall mark him well –
The Devil screams, he knows he's lost
To Shirtless Stephen of the Cross.

Under the Kurdish stars the night
Drapes round the tombs a pallid light
And like the willow in its sleep
A mother hangs her head to weep.

The tamarind shakes out it leaves
And hides the breeze inside its sleeves –
There Sharon's pool is glassed with dust
And Tancred's sword drops flakes of rust.

Come back, you days of Godfrey bold,
Restore the gracious Age of Gold,
And Acre, Gaza, Antioch
Rejoice again by Zion's Rock.

Now Stephen puts his shirt back on
And teaches you another song
The enemies of God must fall
When children march against their wall.

From Antichrist comes every doubt –
We shatter them with joyful shout
The face of God is lit by war
When cross and Stephen go before.

Their scattered bodies strewn like stones
Their graves unmanned, their harvest, hones;
The children cry across the sea
What was, what is, what still must be.

Stephen's Letter from the Virgin Mary

To my beloved servant, Stephen of the sweet skin: love
your mother who bleaches washing on the stones of St.
Cloud: you must wear your woolly vest when the wind is
high, but when God's sun shines, show your cuttle body to
the world – Stephen, my son, be like your namesake with
the arrows, call the children together and march to Zion.
When you reach the sea, it will remember what it learned
from Moses and split before you – your children will march
on across the gritty miles of ocean till you reach the temple
of the rock. There the angel host has strung it bows. White
will show against the dark, and strike all shadows from the
world.

Stephen's final resolve

Where is Jerusalem? It must be wherever God is,
not on a mound of bones and wild flowers and King
David's camping place, not just a hill two thousand feet
high.It doesn't matter where our steps are headed,
we are set on eternity. They say life is a dream; I shall
make death a dream and heaven a dream and all the world
one single marvellous, transitory dream.

Peter Porter